# ONE-LINERS AND PUNCHLINES 2

### LAUGH NOW THINK NEVER

## AJAI KUMAR NARENDRANATH

**BLUEROSE PUBLISHERS**
India | U.K.

Copyright © Ajai Kumar Narendranath 2025

All rights reserved by author. No part of this publication may be reproduced, stored in a retrieval system or transmitted in any form or by any means, electronic, mechanical, photocopying, recording or otherwise, without the prior permission of the author. Although every precaution has been taken to verify the accuracy of the information contained herein, the publisher assume no responsibility for any errors or omissions. No liability is assumed for damages that may result from the use of information contained within.

BlueRose Publishers takes no responsibility for any damages, losses, or liabilities that may arise from the use or misuse of the information, products, or services provided in this publication.

For permissions requests or inquiries regarding this publication, please contact:

BLUEROSE PUBLISHERS
www.BlueRoseONE.com
info@bluerosepublishers.com
+91 8882 898 898
+4407342408967

ISBN: 978-93-7018-179-3

Cover design: Daksh
Typesetting: Tanya Raj Upadhyay

First Edition: May 2025

# Dedication

To **Achhan, Amma**, my wife **Geetha**, my children **Meenakshi** and **Keshav**, my grandson **Shivaansh**, my son-in-law **Prem**, and to all my friends and readers who believe that life is far better lived with a hearty chuckle and a pocketful of light-hearted moments.

And to **Socrates — dark, short but long, and handsome too** — the charming little guy who will live eternally in our hearts and minds, leaving a trail of wisdom, wags, and witty one-liners.

---

# Acknowledgements

My first book was the result of a long-cherished dream. Its warm reception and kind words from readers around the world filled me with joy and gratitude. The journey to this second book, naturally, came as a seamless continuation — like one witty line following another.

Having retired from the rigours of a full-time career, I finally found myself doing what I loved: travelling, relaxing, reading, and quite importantly… staying happily busy doing absolutely nothing! Together with my wife, we wandered through nearby lanes and distant lands, discovering new cultures, cuisines, and histories. And amidst those journeys — especially within our beautiful little state of Kerala, blessed as it is with natural charm, rich heritage, and lovely people — countless everyday moments sparked ideas that quickly morphed into one-liners.

This book owes its humour to the world around me, to the situations and the simple absurdities of life that come with a subtle, often unintentional, comic tinge.

In my first book, **Socrates the dachshund** made a brief but memorable guest appearance. This time, he's grabbed a plum role, bringing along his feline partner, **Kat**, to add charm, banter, and the occasional insult. **Socrates — dark, short but long, and handsome too — has a way of making**

**his presence felt, and I suspect he always will.**

I remain forever grateful to those who motivated me during my first book's creation. Their guidance continues to light my path. I'd also like to thank my ever-enthusiastic publisher, whose persistent nudges to promote the first book and take the leap towards the second made this possible.

To everyone who smiled, laughed, or paused to think after reading my words — **thank you from the bottom of my heart.**

---

# Preface

I wanted this second book to be not just a continuation, but a step up from the first one. That inspired me to add two lively new characters: **Socrates**, my loving dachshund, and **Kat**, his sharp, feline mate. In this book, you'll find quite a few of their conversations — secretly recorded — covering everything from logic to philosophy, nonsense to outright trash. And, of course, a good sprinkling of wisdom and wit from Socrates himself, occasionally soliloquizing in his unique style.

The rest of the punchlines follow no rules, no sequence, and no order — the only aim is to take the simple and mundane from everyday life and turn them into a chuckle.

You'll notice this book has a more reader-friendly flavour, with puns and wordplay occasionally nudged into italics, helping readers catch the twist a little easier.

Many of these one-liners might not strike resonance immediately — and that's perfectly fine. Savour them. Come back later. The humour will surprise you on the second or third read.

Thank you for joining me on this ride!

---

# About the Author

**Ajai Kumar Narendranath** spent a fulfilling career in construction management. Post-retirement, he chose to build something else entirely — **laughter**.

His lifelong love for writing, which was briefly shelved during the hustle of professional life, found its voice again with the publication of *One-Liners and Punchlines – A Laugh-a-Minute Collection* in 2024. The book earned praise from readers in India and beyond, inspiring this sequel.

In his first book, **Socrates the dachshund** made a charming guest appearance. In this new outing, he returns in a plum role, accompanied by his razor-sharp feline companion, **Kat. Socrates — dark, short but long, and handsome too — now occupies a permanent spot in Ajai's world of one-liners, adding philosophy, nonsense, and no small amount of canine wisdom.**

Ajai lives in Kochi, Kerala with his wife, enjoying a life rich with travel, photography, food, movies, reading, music, gardening, and imaginary conversations with the aforementioned Socrates and Kat. The couple's two children — Meenakshi, married to Prem, with their son Shivaansh, and Keshav — now live abroad, though their voices and laughter remain firmly rooted at home.

❖ I love playing chess with elderly people, but the hardest part is convincing 32 of them to *climb* onto the board!

❖ Socrates: Do you think our owners realize how much we know about them?
Kat: Only when we sit on their keyboards—it's the one time they truly see who's in command... and in control of the mouse!

❖ The sage offered me a boon, so I wished for the ultimate superpower—finding my glasses and car keys instantly every morning!

❖ The busiest day of my week? *'One day*—that's when all my grand plans and big dreams are scheduled.

❖ Masks: The only accessory that makes you look mysterious while keeping your bad breath a secret!

❖ I planned an apartment complex exclusively for detectives - I called it *Sherlock Homes*!

❖ Smelly shoes: the only thing that clears a room faster than a bad joke!

❖ With no porters around, I had no choice but to *carry* my own advice.

- The tongue-twister arrested for murder is expected to get a *long sentence.*

- If I *saw* you tomorrow, does that make you a *split* personality?

- Raavana fainted at the buffet counter when he saw the sign: ₹850 per *head*.

- *Club* culture actually started millions of years ago, when prehistoric man first discovered the art of using *'hit' weapons.*

- Time is precious—*waste* it wisely.

- Socrates, my dachshund, said I'd truly appreciate his height if I saw the world from his perspective—flat-out on the floor!

- I plan to *write a lot on the Taj Mahal*—hope I don't get caught with the spray paint!

- After endless sanitizing, my hands have become hopelessly *alcoholic*!

- My wife wasn't too impressed with my *glass painting* skills—especially after she saw the expensive pair of sunglasses I had just 'finished'!

❖ At the cannibal meeting, I was introduced as a *'man of taste'*—and I couldn't decide whether to be flattered or worried.

❖ '*Count* Dracula!' the jury thundered. He started, '1, 2, 3, 4, 5, 6...'

❖ Saving the planet seems easier than convincing my neighbour to stop burning garbage.

❖ At historical sites, the only thing as old as the monuments is the *vandalism carved* into them.

- We just couldn't see eye to eye—our *fonts* were in completely different styles!

- Socrates: Hands? Not important—it's all about the feet.
Kat: Exactly! Humans wobble on two, but with our four, we've got the upper paw.

- The Sun heaved a sigh of relief after Copernicus' discovery—finally, it could stop running after Earth and let Earth do the orbiting for a change!

❖ I'm not sure if it's a sin, but I obeyed my doctor—took the *sleeping pills* with a glass of water and sent them to their eternal rest!

❖ I was told to *keep an eye* on the kid while my wife went shopping—now he's missing, and I'm down to my last eye searching for him!

❖ Searching for my keys used to be a daily struggle at work—now, in retirement, it's my full-time career!

❖ As a kid, I was afraid of the dark—now, thanks to my electricity bill, I'm downright terrified of the light!

❖ Today I met an alien—he wasn't staring at any *screen*!

❖ Yesterday, I accidentally swallowed some glass when the window shattered on me—now I've got a real pane in the gut!

❖ The accountant visited the psychiatrist, complaining he heard strange *invoices* in his sleep.

❖ My wife came out of the beauty parlour looking so transformed, she hardly recognized me!

❖ I spent days trying to spell '*inconsequential*,' then realized it didn't really matter.

- The only thing my wife wonders about my future is whether I'll age like a fine antique—or just become outdated junk!

- I only drink on special occasions—like whenever my wife's back is turned!

- The spider at home got so terrified by my wife's scream, it had a heart attack—saving her the trouble of squashing it!

- My favourite home workout? Repeatedly lifting the TV remote and punching the keypads—it's a high-intensity, remote-controlled fitness program!

- I played cricket with a bat... and then it flew away!

- My kitchen skills are just like my oven: they only know how to heat things up to '*burnt*!'

- In snake land, the washrooms were labelled '*Hiss*' and '*Hers*'.

- The entry to the skin clinic was decided through a *'scratch and win'* competition.

- I booked an apartment online, and two years later, they handed over an empty space—looks like I now *virtually* own a flat!

❖ Socrates, my dachshund, likes to think of himself as *long, dark, and handsome*—clearly, modesty isn't his strong suit!

❖ In the battlefield, I froze at the shout of '*Mine!*'—turns out, it was just two soldiers battling over the last chocolate bar!

❖ At the wax museum, I was the only one sweating—and everyone thought I was the one *melting*!

❖ I've become so accustomed to my mask that when I took it off, I forgot who I was!

❖ At the government office, while following up on my file, I saw a snail zoom past—proof that even it had a faster chance of getting things done!

❖ I had a *date* last night... sweet, but a bit too dry.

❖ My cooking is like a horror movie—everyone's screaming in terror before the main course even makes its grand entrance!

❖ In the world of tennis, *love* is always a big *zero*.

❖ I went on a roller coaster and discovered that my stomach had a better scream than I do!

- During my teenage years, I was so awkward at announcing my love, I ended up sending a *friend request* instead!

- All my magic tricks start delightfully with "abracadabra"... and end disastrously with "oops!"

- Why clean the house when you can dim the lights and call it *mood lighting*?

- My dachshund Socrates says, "If you can't reach it, bark like it's the apocalypse—someone will rush it to you like it's a national emergency!"

❖ Thanks to social media, I've discovered my neighbour's cat has more followers than I do!

❖ My boss said I was too self-centred, so they got me to *sell fish*—now I'm officially *sel-fish*!

❖ In school, I was so lazy about homework, I considered '*procrastination*' my major!

❖ I failed my driving test when they asked what I do at a red light—and I said, "Check my emails!"

❖ I started trading shares after reading too many comics—now I'm the market's biggest laughing *stock*!

❖ With every house armed with a yellow mosquito racket, mosquitoes might be training a new generation of world-class tennis players—with shocking results!

❖ My bucket list took a hit during a water crisis—my wife took the bucket, ditched the list, and said, "Dream later, store now!"

❖ My dachshund Socrates says, "Remember, it's not the size of the dog in the fight; it's the size of the *heart in the belly*!"

❖ I'm a reluctant rider in my *nightmares*, where the horses of the night take me on wild adventures I never signed up for!

❖ I hired a black magician to turn my white car dark—the shade didn't change, but now it levitates and demands blood sacrifices for fuel.

❖ I soundproofed the house after the neighbours rushed in—my wife screamed at a cockroach, but they thought I was killing her!

❖ Socrates: "Why do humans keep throwing things for us to fetch? It's exhausting."
Kat: "I don't fetch. I delegate."

❖ Starving in the desert, I snapped at my wife—she snapped back so hard, I had to eat my words… surprisingly filling and well-cooked!

❖ Going green is easy and great—until it's time to sort through the recycling bin and realize I'm colour blind!

❖ I thought earthquakes were natural disasters—until my wife discovered online shopping. Now my bank account trembles weekly!

❖ The alumni reunion is the one place you can attend without a disguise and still go unrecognized.

❖ My dachshund Socrates says, "Life's too short to rush—so take your time and sniff those muddy shoes… and anything else that catches your *nose*!"

❖ I brought a large ladder to the party when I heard the drinks were *on the house*—thought I could get *high* on the roof.

❖ I've told my relatives to keep my funeral short and snappy—I'd hate to be bored to death twice!

❖ The pole vault champ got so rich, he now practices on a gold vault—his only competition is Fort Knox!

❖ I'm trying to go green, but my *carbon footprint* keeps stomping all over my efforts!

❖ With an MBA, I don't do housekeeping—I practice *strategic dust management*!

❖ After reading too many comics, I now only speak in *speech bubbles*!

❖ Cricket is a *bird-friendly* game—played with *bats*, packed with *ducks*, and the *Kiwis* always flock together for a strong innings!

❖ The guy at the petrol station was so rustic and arrogant—he was a real *crude oil dispenser*!

- ❖ I gave my team enough rope to make a decision—now we've got a full-fledged Tug of War League with team jerseys and sponsors!

- ❖ Socrates: The world's a big place—but the biggest crisis? Humans forgetting belly rubs.
Kat: True! If only they scrolled less and scratched more, world peace might be possible.

- ❖ To help the training group shed their inhibitions, I introduced an ice-breaking session — didn't realize I'd trigger a climate crisis!

- ❖ A building is never truly complete because it's always '*building*'.

❖ My boss asked me to get a kilo of nails for the construction site—so I'm collecting them from horror movie audiences busily biting theirs!

❖ My procrastinator's calendar has two pages: '*Today*,' which is always *blank*, and '*Tomorrow*,' which is perpetually *overbooked*!

❖ Count Dracula walked into the bank and made a withdrawal—from the necks of depositors, with a *bite* of interest, naturally!

❖ If you *saw* everything, don't be surprised when the blade files a complaint for overwork!

❖ At the alumni re-union, I wandered into the wrong batch, wrong course—maybe even the wrong college. Still walked away with "Most Regular Attendee"!

❖ When a Nigerian scammer asked for money, I gave him my Somalian uncle's widow's email—she's been trying to send me millions for years. Let them sort it out themselves. Win-win for everyone!

❖ When my kids were little, they called the ATM "Appa the Magician"— I'd swipe my card, and money popped out like magic!

❖ I used to stash vodka in mineral water bottles to dodge my wife's sharp eye—until I noticed the level dropping and her spirits lifting!

❖ I went to repay my loan, but the financier threw me out—turns out, he doesn't accept *money plants* as legal tender!

❖ At the mall, I saw a sign that said "Wet Floor!"—so I helpfully splashed more water around. Just doing my bit for accurate signage!

❖ When my wife asks me to do the dishes, I instantly turn into *Supermoan.*

- Socrates: This AI can analyze data faster than I chase my tail!
Kat: Big deal. I'll stick to warm laps over cold algorithms—at least until it can purr and knock mugs off tables.

- In the confession chamber, I confessed to the eagerly curious priest all the *typo errors* I made this week. He advised me to switch off *autocorrect* and reduce my sins.

- To cut a long story short—I took inspiration from the French guillotine. Now my editor sleeps with one eye open.

- Chemistry tells me Iron Man is actually *Fe-male*.

❖ After the argument, my wife inspected me so closely, I thought she was checking for an expiry date—just to see if it was time to toss me out!

❖ My business guru said I needed two cranes to break into construction—so I got two birds, built a pond, stocked it with fish… and now I'm just wondering why the contracts aren't flying in.

❖ The Dalmatian I bought on the cheap shed its spots in the rain—guess I paid for paint, not pedigree!

❖ See the trees, *saw* only when absolutely required.

❖ I bought *bird seed* the other day—planted it in the backyard and now I'm just waiting for the parrots to bloom.

❖ Socrates: Life insurance is important, Kat.
Kat: I tried, but the agent fainted when I asked if they offer "Buy 1, Cover *9* plans!"

❖ I placed an ad for a math tutor—next morning, an adder slithered in with a chalkboard and hissed, "Let's multiply!"

❖ I got hospitalized after being kicked by a horse—on the bright side, my condition is now *stable*!

❖ Socrates: I watched my human struggle to build that toy—I could've done it faster with paws and no thumbs.
Kat: Naturally, they couldn't build it… I'd already chewed the instructions.

❖ The masseurs held a press conference to *press* their demands for better working conditions—talk about using pressure tactics!

❖ I cheated at music school and ended up in some serious *treble*.

❖ My cookery book fell into the boiling pot—now I'm sipping *papyrus* stew seasoned with a hundred soggy recipes!

- Me: I started writing a book called *The Seven Habits of Highly Lazy People*—but after chapter one, I took a well-earned lifetime break.
  Socrates: You wrote a chapter? Overachiever.
  Kat: Naturally. He stopped once he realised turning pages counts as exercise.

- Life after marriage? *Speechless*!

- Seeing the goon, I drew my gun. Though he wasn't very impressed with my skills, he still asked me to draw one for him too!

❖ The police put out a lookout notice for a six-foot man who stole three pairs of shoes—public's now on high alert for a well-dressed insect!

❖ My socks have become so *holey*, I kneel in prayer every time I see them.

❖ I dumped all my household waste into the computer's *Recycle Bin*, but it didn't process—so much for a high-end machine that can't even handle my simple trash!

❖ Forgetfulness is the only thing I don't need to remember every day.

- Socrates: "I'm not short—I'm a limited-edition sausage with a tail and self-esteem!"
Kat: "Self-esteem? Last week you barked at your reflection for 10 minutes."

- The police raided my house for storing *radioactive* material—turns out it was just my paying guest, an *FM radio jockey* with highly charged energy!

- My dachshund Socrates says, 'I may be built low and long, but hey, that just means I'm first in line for all the best smells!'

- Thomas Edison looked at a heavy candle and thought, 'Too many calories—let's invent a light bulb.'

- The Sphinx: "Centuries of standing still for photos, and not a single complaint!"

Tower of Pisa: "Lucky you—I've been stuck in a permanent *lean*, and people think it's charming!"

- *Geology* rocks—I'm leaving no stone unturned… except the lazy ones, they can sit there and sediment!

- How well glass coffins preserve bodies *remains to be seen*!

❖ I hide all my passwords in a *home appliances manual*—I've hardly seen anyone open one, not even out of curiosity!

❖ To improve my grammar, I started studying the *Comma Sutra*—it's all about mastering the right pause for the perfect sentence!

❖ My car has a child lock feature—I'm convinced only the kids know how to work it!

❖ The only time politicians lie is when they open their mouths.

❖ I've decided to switch to the metric system—*inch by inch*.

❖ The only thing harder than finding old friends at the reunion was pretending I was thrilled to see them again!

❖ As an environmental freak, the first thing on my bucket list is... well, a bucket—eco-friendly, biodegradable, and preferably judging me for using water.

❖ At the art festival, I drew a blank. They said it captured the void of modern life—I say I forgot my pencil.

❖ I attended the meeting representing the *camouflage* unit—turns out, I was marked absent. Mission accomplished!

❖ Whenever AI comes up, my wife just points at me and says, 'Living proof—heavy on the artificial, light on the intelligence!'

❖ Socrates: "*Miss Universe*? Please. I've sniffed every inch of Earth, and not once have I met a contestant from Jupiter."
Kat: "Exactly. Until Venus sends a diva and Mars brings a makeup artist, it's just *Miss World* with delusions of grandeur."
Alien (beaming in): "We tried competing once—your judges thought our antennae were costume malfunctions."

❖ As an engineer, I solve complex problems—mostly *simple ones* I've expertly *overengineered* into structural disasters.

❖ I'm planning a *facelift*, and all the major elevator companies have submitted their quotes.

❖ I thought *out of the box*—now I can't figure out which one to get back into!

❖ Socrates: "When it comes to CAPTCHAs, I bet ChatGPT would fail." Kat: "Of course it would. AI may be smart, but it still can't tell a fire hydrant from a mailbox—or pet me properly."

❖ I've been getting praised for my amazing piano notes creating magic with the audience—turns out, it's just my cat running all over the keys!

❖ Socrates: At the end of the day, we're the real rulers of this kingdom, right?
Kat: Absolutely! They pay the bills, and we reign supreme from our thrones of cushions, demanding belly rubs!

❖ My doctor said I had a weak heart, so I asked for a *second opinion*—he told me my kidneys were bad too!

❖ When the Invisible Man died, nobody noticed.

❖ I started eating *pi*, and now I can't stop—it's literally a never-ending snack!

❖ I *spotted* a mongrel and sold him as a Dalmatian—now the plain white cat wants *stripes* to become a tiger, and my neighbour's horse is having an identity crisis, dreaming of being a *zebra*!

❖ The most dangerous room in my house? Whichever one my wife is in!

❖ My foot is *numb* from the cold… 567 is *number*.

- ❖ After taking the *Pfizer* vaccine, I'm pfeeling absolutely pfine—and a little pflattered by all the attention!

- ❖ Meet the visionary who transformed '*nothing*' into a revolutionary concept—*zero*'s inventor made emptiness truly count!

- ❖ Creating *headlines* is easy—just furrow your brow and let people assume you're thinking deep thoughts!"

- ❖ I'm terrified of meeting Mammootty—he's in his seventies and still a superstar. What if he calls *me* uncle?

- ❖ Socrates: "I timed my human's shower—long enough to write a novel and cause a drought!"
Kat: "Too bad. I clean myself with a lick and a glare. Humans need a tail to swish some sense into them!"

- ❖ The room was so crowded, I could barely *stretch my imagination*—creativity had to squeeze in sideways!

- ❖ My dachshund Socrates says: I got kicked out of the police dog squad for *barking up the wrong tree*!

- ❖ To stay healthy, I make sure to *exercise my options* from time to time!

- Vegan cannibals only eat *human beans.*

- All national anthems are just *country* music.

- I joined a secret cooking society, but they kicked me out for *spilling the beans.*

- Grumbling by nature, I was always a *homegroan* boy.

- I used to think greed, jealousy, and materialism were bad… but then I *gave up thinking*—problem solved!

- The Titanic had a *kitchen sink* in the pantry before it *sank* into icy waters.

- If dinosaurs existed today, they'd still go extinct—climate change, pollution, deforestation… and someone would've opened an all-you-can-eat dino buffet!

- When it comes to charity, some people stop at *nothing*.

- Better to see the spider than wonder where it went—at least then you can negotiate terms before abandoning your house!

- I crossed a couple of cheques as practice before attempting to cross the damaged bridge—safety first!

❖ My doctor says the body is 80% water—so in this heat, I sleep with one eye open in case I evaporate overnight!

❖ I got so hooked on math, they sent me to a de-addition centre—now I'm subtracting the habit and multiplying my peace of mind!

❖ The hottest girls on Earth? Geography students have known for ages — it's always sizzling near the Equator!

❖ I'm great at making a *lasting impression*—I stamp *seals* on documents for a living.

❖ My dachshund Socrates says, 'Life's a long walk—just remember to stop, mark your territory, and assert dominance like you own every lamppost in town!

❖ People are *shocked* when they find out I'm a terrible electrician.

❖ And this year's Anuratna Award—the Oscars of the bacteria world—goes to the 0.01% of germs that hand sanitizer *couldn't* kill. They've survived ethanol, soap, and shame. Legends!

❖ They promoted me from 24/7 to 25/8—my co-worker's still stuck on 9 to 5 and plotting revenge with HR!

❖ The Potbellies Association calls their annual meet the "Maha Kumbh Mela"—a *circumferential confluence* of expanding waistlines!

❖ A *sound* engineer doesn't need to know acoustics—any engineer with a fat bank balance is already making music to their ears!

❖ My wife, with her *mud pack* on, gave me a dirty look.

❖ That joke had me in *splits*—by the time I put myself back together, I was walking on my hands and clapping with my feet!

- I don't tell jokes to lazy people—they just refuse to work!

- In places where beef is banned, I switched my car horn from *'beep beep'* to 'honk honk'—didn't want to get grilled for it!

- I dropped my ATM PIN—if you find four sharp little digits on the floor, don't try picking them up... you might get pricked!

- In the polar courts of law, don't expect much—*just- ice* and *cold, hard* evidence!

❖ I had to write an essay on an elephant—tried doing it directly on its back, but the wrinkles kept ruining my handwriting!

❖ Socrates says, 'Good friends are like buried bones—rare, treasured, and worth digging up the whole yard for!'

❖ I showed the spider a mirror—it ran off screaming, probably thinking, "Help! A *hairy-legged freak* is after me!"

❖ Pilots: the only professionals who can *take off* while doing their duty!

❖ I read so much about the dangers of smoking, drinking, and drugs… I finally quit reading. Too risky!

❖ I *take* great photos wherever I go—mainly because no one's noticed I'm stealing them. The big framed ones are tricky to sneak out!

❖ I live in constant fear—the boomerang I threw away long ago still hasn't returned!

❖ At the top of my '10 things to do before you die' list is yell for a doctor.

- ❖ I thought James Bond was a type of glue—spent weeks wondering why MI6 needed such strong adhesive!

- ❖ I held myself close to a candle to burn fat—talk about a *light* workout.

- ❖ I read my wife's horoscope to find out how *my* day is going to be.

- ❖ My wife dragged me to an *artificial intelligence* exhibition the other day—turns out, I was one of the exhibits!

- ❖ I'm so illiterate, I thought "reading glasses" were just spectacles that read *to you*.

❖ Greek history has always been my weakness—my Achilles' foot!

❖ Peace and harmony reigned at home—until I saved my wife's extra SIM as '*Wife2*.

❖ I walked into the bank and asked to check my *balance*—they just pushed me over!

❖ If all countries were ruled by women, there'd be no wars—just peace talks and endless gossip!

❖ To make *small things* count, I started teaching *little kids* math!

- During COVID, I discovered my most vital organ—*my ears*! Without them, my mask would've just been a confused napkin flapping in the breeze!

- Socrates: "Procrastination saved my life—every time I planned to give up, I just postponed it."
Kat: "Honestly, your to-do list is a suicide note crossed out daily."

- I asked if I could take her home—she said yes. Now, I'm busy finalizing the *sale deed* for her house!

- Message near the water tap: Save water, or *drops* dead.

❖ I use my shin bone to identify hard objects in the dark—who needs a flashlight when you have your own built-in sound effects?

❖ Socrates: Man created the catwalks, and crabs the sidewalks. Kat: And if they ever swap lanes, it's going to be a real *claws-tastrophe*!

❖ While running cross-country, exhausted, I wave my *shirt* at the speeding cars—while the dog *pants*!

❖ These days, some people consult Dr. Google first, then visit a real doctor for a second opinion—just to make sure the diagnosis is as wild as their search history!

❖ My son asked me to perform a magic trick by tossing my smartphone into the river—poof! I instantly turned into a vegetable… now I'm just a *couch potato*!

❖ At the bar, I raised two fingers and the bartender brought two beers. My *Roman* friend raised two fingers and got five beers—still don't get the math!

❖ My wife finally found the letters I was hiding… now we're back to fighting over triple word scores in *Scrabble*!

❖ I tripped over a pile of beans—*rest in peas.*

❖ Socrates: Humans are head over heels for AI these days. We've been practising it for generations!
Kat: Exactly! They're still miles away from the original AI—*Animal Intelligence.*

❖ I got too close to the beehive, walked into a honey trap, and ended up in a sting operation—guess I was *buzzed* for all the wrong reasons!

❖ Cello tape is a brilliant invention—until you realize the starting point needs patient fingers and divine intervention.

❖ At the supermarket, I picked up an insecticide and asked, 'Is it good for mosquitoes?' The clerk replied, ''For you, yes. For them, it's their worst nightmare!

❖ Thinking outside the box, I realized the box seriously needed a fresh coat of paint—guess even creativity needs a touch-up!

❖ With a *couple of bulges* around the middle, I'm definitely *centrefold* material— in the 'Before' section of a fitness ad!

❖ I keep forgetting to tell my doctor about my amnesia—guess it's a memory lapse!

❖ Trying to escape through a 20th-floor window, the cops grabbed my leg—turns out I was the wrong guy, so they did the right thing and *let me go*!

❖ If I'm doing everything *right* all the time, there must be something seriously wrong with me!

❖ I'm extra careful with my new toothpaste—it says *'extra sensitive,'* and I don't want to *hurt its feelings*!

❖ I loaned my friend a fortune for his *plastic surgery*—now he's nowhere to be seen, and I have no idea what he looks like!

- My neighbour spies on me—I caught him Googling my name while I was watching him do it… through *my* telescope!

- He adds up so fast, I'm convinced we're going to have a sizzling *summer*.

- I tried thinking outside the box, but once I got out, I gave up on thinking and went *sightseeing* instead!

- Still don't get why I was arrested— when the policeman said, "*Papers*," I instantly replied, "*Scissors*!"

❖ Socrates: Humans invented entire languages to bark commands at us—yet somehow "feed me" in tail wags still needs translation!
Kat: Right? After centuries together, and they still haven't cracked the code of a meow that means "Now, not later!"

❖ A clever theft with no fingerprints? Now that's a *stainless* steal!

❖ My confidence in real estate dropped so low, I ended up building an inferiority *complex*!

❖ I got caught red-handed while robbing the blood bank.

❖ I decided to kill off a few characters in my new book—turns out, it's my *autobiography*!

❖ When my guest asked who uses my vast library, I introduced him to my reading glasses!

❖ The only cardio I get these days is running out of money.

❖ My wife stopped insisting I kill spiders when I told her they'd come back as creepy little ghosts.

❖ Sloths, pandas, grizzlies— all part of the Ursidae family—filled the room until it was completely *un-bear-able*!

❖ During Covid, I was asked to identify my wife from a group of ladies without masks—I failed miserably. Then they put on the masks, and there she was!

❖ They came to the tennis academy, saw how well I *serve*, and next thing I knew, I was appointed head waiter!

❖ The main downside of polygamy? Too many mothers-in-law!

❖ He who smiles when things go wrong has already found someone else to blame.

❖ I'm so poor, I can't even afford to *pay* attention!

❖ My neighbour has an Audi, and I have... a cataract—guess who's really seeing the future?

❖ I was snoring so loud while driving that the passengers started protesting!

❖ I'm a down-to-earth person—though with this belly, I bounce before I touch ground!

❖ The guys chasing Iron Man turned out to be scrap dealers!

❖ The fuel price hike was announced by the petroleum *monster*—and no, that's not a typo error.

❖  At the riverbank, I saw a sign that said, 'Watch for crocodiles.' Guess they've really mastered telling time now!

❖  The other day, the police complimented my driving—they even left a note on my windshield that said, 'Parking fine'!

❖  At a teaching job interview, they asked about my experience—I said, 'I taught a lesson just the other day… to the guy who wouldn't shut up on his phone at the movies!

❖  At the leadership camp, the trainer said, 'Go forth.' So, I let the other three go first.

❖ The fight broke out when I tucked my wife into bed and sincerely said, 'Rest in peace'—turns out, timing matters!

❖ I bought a pair of Chinese reading glasses the other day—still can't read Chinese!

❖ Today, I watched the world's first silent movie—couldn't understand a thing, and the subtitles were missing too!

❖ My dream of bungee jumping off the edge of the Earth was crushed by Eratosthenes—guess the world's just not flat enough!

❖ Dressed as Birdman, I was the first to reach the party— they gifted me a box of worms.

❖ After the Kleptomaniacs Anonymous meeting, the room was empty—including all the furniture!

❖ The menu said 'breakfast *anytime*,' so I ordered idlis from the Chola period.

❖ I told my new travel buddy I used to be scared of ghosts. 'Me too,' he said, 'when I was *alive*.'

❖ Are heavy metal bands called that because they all have a *lead* guitar?

❖ They promised to make me years younger in a day—so they changed my birthday to *February 29*!

❖ It gives me the creeps knowing there's a skeleton inside me... just waiting for the right moment to *walk* out on me!

❖ I have no clue who my great-grandfather was—proof that four generations from now, I'll be just as *memorable* as a blank page!

❖ I went to a *second-hand* store and bought one. Now there's a stranger's hand in my pocket, and I have no idea who it's waving at!

❖ The government's tender to produce their signature product—*red tape*—has been delayed, ironically, by *red tape*!

❖ My age is just the number of times I've circled the sun—making me a globe-trotter, and a slap in the face to anyone who calls me a couch potato!

❖ I think the word 'queue' is a waste—it could've just been one letter, the other four are just standing in line, clueless about why they're even there!

- Raavana's business card reads 'Branch Heads'—probably multitasking at a whole new level!

- Socrates: My owner thinks I'm just a pet, but I'm basically their emotional support system!
Kat: Exactly! They come to us for comfort, but we should be charging them a *pet* fee for our services!

- Lost my diary today, so my thoughts are with someone else now—looks like they'll be *me* for a while!

- I always feared *division* in math—then religion and politics showed me how surprisingly easy it is!

- Thanks to my *origami* skills, I managed to unfold the mystery... one crease at a time!

- I'm waiting for my dream job—the one where my only duty is to sit, dream, and get a paycheck!

- The builder asked how high I had built, and I said 51 *stories*—he wanted to hear more.

- At the expo, I set up an empty cage labelled *'The Invisible Man'*—and people couldn't stop staring at pure air like it was the main attraction!

- If God's watching, let's at least not bore Him!

❖ To prove I'm a sharpshooter, I shoot first and fix the target later—I prefer to call it 'creative accuracy'!

❖ People say I spread happiness wherever I go… mostly when I *leave* the room!

❖ The branding iron—an invention that really left its *mark* on everyone!

❖ Behind every angry woman, there's a man—most likely hiding for his life!

❖ In India, we truly believe *zebra crossings* are meant for zebras—pedestrians treat them like forbidden territory!

❖ I went to the shop to buy invisible ink—paid a hefty price, and the guy handed me an empty bottle. Best purchase I never saw!

❖ Socrates: Does a good liar go to heaven?
Kat: If he's really good, he'll talk his way past Saint Peter!

❖ My wife scared me so much about my loud snores, I bought earplugs—now I can sleep through both my snoring and her complaints!

❖ At the shooting championships, I hit the *bull's-eye*—now animal activists are hot on my heels, with me as their new target!

❖ Life depends a lot on proper '*whether*' conditions—especially when it's raining decisions and you can't decide if you need an umbrella or a raincoat!

❖ They told me to take a taxi on my way back—I did, and now I'm being charged with theft... I only followed orders!

❖ I sent a cheque to the bank, and they returned it saying *'Insufficient Funds'*—didn't realize things were that rough on their end!

❖ Thought outside the box and found it completely worn out—looks like I need a *fresh box of ideas*!

❖ The Internet—the ultimate weapon of *mass distraction*, where productivity goes to die, cat videos stage a coup, and conspiracy theories get PhDs!

❖ Nursing a black eye, I played 'I Spy with my little eye'—though I only saw blurry blobs and the punch that found me!

❖ I tried thinking laterally, but all I did was grow horizontally—looks like I'm literally an *all-rounder* now!

❖ I miss my wife so much, I started taking sharpshooter classes—figured it's the only way I'll ever get *close* to her again!

❖ I thought my name was unique—until every username I tried to create *uniquely was* already taken by 47 others!

❖ My IQ must be off the charts—I finished a 30-piece jigsaw in 5 hours, even though the box said *5-7 years*! Might tackle the *3-4* years next and crush it in 2 hours!

❖ Adam's Apple and Lady's Finger—proof that even cannibals have *vegetarian* options on the menu!

❖ Withdrawal symptoms disappear as soon as your bank deposits run dry!

❖ What came first, the chicken or the egg? First came the question—then came the endless debates!

❖ He became a billionaire selling scrap steel—*rust* is history!

❖ I told my friends my bucket list includes world travel—they suggested I start with my local grocery store, as a *first step* towards longer journeys!

❖ My wife says I ruined her birthday—I don't get it, I didn't even *know* it was her birthday!

❖ In tough times, stick to horses—at least it's a stable job!

❖ I gave my shadow too much freedom—now it struts like *I'm* the one following *it*!

❖ The internet's full of scams, but for just ₹999.95, I'll teach you how to dodge them—limited offer, no refunds!

❖ I got a job as a waiter at the *Hotel California*—great perks, friendly staff, but yeah... *you can never leave!*

❖ Whenever I'm alone, I realize I'm in *the worst* company!

❖ While searching for my lost wallet, I ended up losing my mind too.

- The tallest guy in the theatre? Oh, he's easy to spot—just look for the one sitting right in front of *me*, blocking my view!

- The Genie promised me shapely *figures* for company, and *poof!* — I'm stuck staring at an Excel sheet carrying financial *numbers*!

- I went to a 'buy one, get one free' sale—now I've got 11 with me. What do I do with them?

- I logged my meal into a fitness app—next thing I know, an ambulance shows up with sirens blazing!

- After you die, you're no longer a human *being*—just a human *been*!

- I wrote letters to everyone I hated and burned *them*—now I'm stuck wondering what to do with the letters.

- My wife says I never listen to her… or at least that's what I *think* she said.

- My wife is fearless—as long as the spider stays on *its* side of the glass panel!

- I work as a product tester in a chloroform factory—being *unconscious* is the job!

- ❖ I asked for *speakers* for my sound system, and the taxi took me to *Toastmasters*—now I've got zero bass but a booming stage presence!

- ❖ Socrates: What do you mean by a win-win situation? I've heard humans mention it often.
  Kat: Oh, that's when *both* sides pretend they didn't lose!

- ❖ After death, heaven or hell? Depends on Wi-Fi availability—no signal, no paradise!

- ❖ I thought about getting my brain checked... but then I changed my mind.

❖ Socrates: "Hey Kat, it's Mother's Day — finally her turn to be spoiled!" Kat: "Yeah, after a year of cleaning our mess, I say we let her nap on our cushions for once! But only for today. Tomorrow, those cushions are back under *royal* occupation!"

❖ Of all mammals, seals definitely know how to make a lasting *impression.*

❖ I knew I was in cannibal country when I walked into a restaurant and heard, 'Look who's on the menu!

❖ The hottest spot in the room? The corners—they're always a scorching *90 degrees*!

- I'll never forgive my wife... if she catches *me* cheating!

- The bank asked for proof of residence—like *dragging* my house to them every time isn't tiring enough!

- Election time? I'm only loyal to the *parties* that come with music and snacks on the weekend!

- My room's such a mess, even a nuclear attack wouldn't make a difference!

- The doctor says I can't sleep well—apparently, I'm running a serious '*zzzzzzz*' deficit!

❖ Being *lion-hearted* got me promptly detained at the zoo.

❖ I fell for a philosopher—she says I'm just a figment of my own imagination!

❖ Consciousness: the annoying intermission between quality naps!

❖ My conversations are like 'banananananana'—no clue when to stop the na-nsense!

❖ The maternity hospital advertised for delivery experts—then got flooded with *courier company resumes*!

❖ Socrates: "Why do they call it a 'smart home'? Shouldn't a truly wise home just have more comfy spots to lounge?"

Kat: "Exactly! Who needs a fridge that talks back when you could have a window that opens itself when life gets stuffy?"

❖ My neighbour's so rich, he didn't just buy his dog a toy—he hired a *boy* to play with him!

❖ Divorces don't just have a cost of living—they hit you with a massive cost of *leaving*!

- At the painting competition, contestants were told to *draw* their own conclusions!

- Prisoners love punctuation—especially the period, because it ends their *sentence*!

- I quit writing my autobiography after my wife read it and asked, 'Who's this supposed to be about?'

- I got her a gift no one can *beat*—a broken drum!

- A friend asked how much I spend on a bottle of wine—I said, 'About 15 minutes'.

❖ My neighbour refuses to talk anymore—he's all *write* now!

❖ I went to a web designer's award ceremony—got seated next to a *tarantula*.

❖ Socrates: "The animal world rules the stock markets with *bulls and bears*."
Kat: "Well, they should've hired *dogs and cats*—at least they'd know how to fetch profits and purr through crashes!"

❖ Photography was no laughing matter—until someone said '*cheese*,' and everyone couldn't stop grinning!

- ❖ When the perfume factory shut down for maintenance, they posted a sign: 'Temporarily Out of *Odour*!'

- ❖ Riding a horse in the middle of the night can be a dreadful nightmare.

- ❖ I was named the best web developer, but the spiders disqualified me—they said I needed eight legs to be fully qualified!

- ❖ I started with 'I *think*...' and my wife hasn't stopped laughing since—I'm still trying to figure out what's so funny!

❖ I checked my bank account—my wife's birthday gift is a hug, and my return gift? Definitely a black eye!

❖ At the mind readers' convention, the speaker paused halfway — apparently, the collective silent cursing got a bit too loud.

❖ The owner wanted a spacious *reading* room—so I covered every wall, the ceiling, and the floor in graffiti. Now they can read in any direction!

❖ Tender documents mature into tough contracts!

❖ In corporate circles, *anger management* is the new rage—HR is fighting tooth and nail with the higher-ups just to organize the training!

❖ As an airline pilot, I decided to *work from home* today—passengers aren't thrilled, and my neighbours are panicking about a runway in my backyard!

❖ Why did the chicken cross the road? It finally felt safe after spotting a *zebra* crossing!

❖ As long as I've got a tennis club in hand, no one dares pick a fight with me.

- Kat: It's called a catwalk for a reason—grace is in my genes. Socrates: Sure, but I've got the dogged determination to steal the show!

- YouTube Brutus—where betrayal goes viral with a stabbing twist!

- I started as a floor manager at the new company—turns out, that meant a broom and a bucket!

- My neighbour is being punished for something he didn't do—wipe his fingerprints off the knife!

- Dumb people, smartphones!

- Abroad, I met dogs named Rolex and Timex—true watch dogs. Inspired, I came back to India and named mine HMT!

- He was obsessed with every lead actress—a true *heroine addict*!

- Crowds lined up for guillotine tester jobs—the pay was great, but the *severance* package was a real head-turner!

- Archaeologists are still baffled by how the Pharaohs built the pyramids—they just can't give a *concrete* explanation!

- The caveman signalled, 'We need to talk.' The cavewoman nodded and said, 'I'll show you how.' And that's how the world's first one-way conversation began!

- During COVID, my best friend sent me a heartfelt thank-you note—for skipping his daughter's wedding!

- The audio recording studio installed a bathroom for me—finally, I can sing naturally.

- My dachshund Socrates says, "Parenting is like training a dog—patience, treats, and a lot of 'no' before the good stuff!

- I love autocorrect—my wife wanted 24-carat gold for her birthday, but by the time her message reached me, it said 24 carrots. I happily showed up with a bunch—she wasn't amused, but the rabbit was thrilled!

- The publisher was so squeaky clean, his dictionary didn't have a single four-letter word—not even "word"!

- If we had more suicide bombers, we'd soon have a lot fewer suicide bombers!

- Marriages are made in heaven—the rest are mass-produced in China!

❖ My son wanted to see Iron Man, so I took him to the basement and introduced him to Muthu from Madurai—our laundry superhero, pressing dignity into every dress!

❖ I gave my dachshund Complan—now he thinks he's as tall as a Doberman, has no complaints to bark about, and even looks down on me!

❖ I single-handedly lowered the crime rate—by not getting caught! No medals for that, though.

❖ I gave up exercise—burning fat releases $CO_2$, and I refuse to speed up global warming!

❖ Socrates: My owner thinks they're training me—little do they know, I'm the one in charge!
Kat: Please, we're just extras in their sitcom. They think they're the stars, but we know who runs the show!

❖ My wife told me to add chilli powder to the shopping list—so I did. *Rubbing* it on was a fiery mistake!

❖ After waiting forever for the séance to start, I became the undisputed *medium wait* champion!

❖ I have a terrible memory—which is great, because I sleep like a baby and forget all my worries!

❖ Two's company, three's a crowd, four's a boundary, five's a stampede, and six? That's a sixer—knocking it out of the park!

❖ My dachshund Socrates says, "Self-care is like a good ear scratch—essential for a happy life!"

❖ My worst nightmare? Losing my prescription glasses—because I need them to find them!

❖ A manuscript dated 28 B.C. proves fake internet messages existed even back then—history's first spam scroll!

❖ Landed a work-from-home job—now I just need a home to work from!

❖ In this age of nepotism, politicians aren't getting heatstroke—they're getting '*son*'stroke!

❖ Since I did nothing yesterday, I can proudly report today that there are no tasks unfinished!

❖ As an offshore drilling specialist, I told my fiancée, 'Love is so *boring*, dear — it drilled straight to the bottom of my heart.' That was our last conversation. Apparently, metaphors involving industrial equipment aren't as romantic as I thought.

❖ I lost my electrician... *wire* they always so hard to find?

- They told me to fix my stammer—I was just narrating my *great-great-great*-grandfather's life story!

- Hand sanitizer won't help when you're caught red-handed!

- As a kleptomaniac, I once walked into an empty room... and still managed to steal a nap!

- My wife reported the remote missing—when they asked for a description, she just showed them my photo!

- When my wife called me flamboyant, I almost spilled my drink—right off my golden throne!

- The dental student who dropped out went from learning about gums to selling adhesives—still sticking to the topic!

- When the autocorrect inventor passed away, my condolence message read: "Rest in piss."

- Lately, I think I'm turning into an Arab—I've started thinking from right to left!

- Socrates: My owner keeps talking about getting fit—I'm all for it if it means more park walks!
Kat: Ha! Mine thinks vacuuming counts as exercise. I call that a tragic waste of prime napping time!

❖ My dachshund Socrates says, "All bark and no bite just makes a dog a yapping disgrace!"

❖ I put a stick in our non-stick pan—now I'm stuck dealing with my wife!

❖ The bar is 10 minutes from my house—but somehow, my house is 2 hours from the bar!

❖ Socrates: "They're making AI that talks to pets—finally, I can complain about the food!"
Kat: "And I can file my demands directly with the Chief Snack Officer!"

❖ I was convicted due to a lakh of evidence.

- ❖ My son wanted to see Spider-Man, so I took him to his mom. She pointed at a spider on the wall, handed me a broom, and he just nodded—lesson learned!

- ❖ My boss said 'failure' wasn't in his dictionary—I told him to sue the publisher immediately!

- ❖ My antidepressants got stolen—someone's out there feeling happier than me!

- ❖ I'm no Picasso, but the only thing I love to draw is my salary!

- ❖ James Bond first worked in adhesives—he always stuck to his assignments!

- At the quick-draw pistol competition, I barely finished sketching my gun before getting shot!

- The light at the end of the tunnel? Turns out it happens to be a train coming my way!

- I've found the secret to a zero-cost life—just move into a cemetery, free rent forever!

- The worst part of being alone? No one else to blame—just me, and I'm not taking responsibility!

- On the cannibal menu, there were no milkshakes—just *handshakes*, and I'm not sure they were friendly!

❖ My dachshund Socrates says, "Online dating is like sniffing other dogs—mostly disappointing, with quite a few awkward moments thrown in!"

❖ Autocorrect: turning my perfectly crafted messages into poetic disasters since forever—I *hat* it.

❖ Socrates: Have you seen those robot vacuum cleaners? They're like the world's most confused dog, bumping into everything!
Kat: That little dust-gobbling traitor tried to steal my sunshine—I've been plotting its downfall ever since!

- "I don't want to go to school!" she cried—after much coaxing, my wife, the teacher, finally got ready.

- Life is all about adjustments—when I mess up, I say sorry. When she messes up... I still say sorry.

- My wife complained I never take her anywhere, so I told her we're off to the Islets of Langerhans—now she's packing a swimsuit!

- The real difference between dogs and cats in their relationships with humans? Dogs have masters—cats have a dedicated staff.

- ❖ I'm convinced doors exist purely as a grand setup for knock-knock jokes.

- ❖ My mom asked if I'd seen the dog bowl—who knew he had a talent for cricket?

- ❖ Tried thinking outside the box, but there was no Wi-Fi out there—so I crawled right back.

- ❖ Chloroform has a *faint* smell—no wonder people become unconscious!

- ❖ Thinking outside the box, I soon spotted the private eye my wife had engaged to track my every move!

❖ Before handing over a stool sample, make sure to ask—are they from a furniture store or a medical lab?

❖ What came first, the chicken or the egg? Entirely depends on the courier's efficiency!

❖ A credit card has three dimensions: length, width, and an ever-growing debt!

❖ Too much food goes to waist—making me a successful all-rounder!

❖ Thanks to Facebook, my wife and I have finally started liking each other.

- ❖ I'm reading a book on the history of glue—so gripping, I simply can't put it down!

- ❖ Despite a twisted ankle, I still finished the race—thanks to my unstoppable running nose!

- ❖ Socrates, my dachshund, says: 'Fashion trends are like bad smells—they fade away, but classics, like a good collar, always stick around!'

- ❖ My New Year's resolution? High definition—2048 x 1536 pixels!

- ❖ Syntax: the penalty one pays for committing disorderly grammatical sins.

- ❖ Here lies the inventor of the time machine: born in 1955, died in 1877—quite ahead of his time, or perhaps behind it.

- ❖ My Eskimo friend invited us to his igloo for a housewarming party—now he's homeless!

- ❖ An hourglass—proof that time has a dangerously slim waist and is fully qualified to enter any beauty pageant!

- ❖ I tried to pay with a card, but apparently, the Six of Spades isn't considered "credit-worthy"!

- Any proper dictionary should have a mistake—if not, someone needs to have a word with the publisher!

- At my IKEA interview, they handed me a chair kit and said, "Take a seat".

- My dachshund, Socrates, insists he holds the key to success—because, as he puts it, success always begins with small steps!

- I'm immensely proud of my unparalleled humility—truly, no one does modesty better than me!

❖ I told the loan shark 'Bear with me' while requesting an extension—haven't heard back since. Guess he's waiting for me to lose the wildlife!

❖ At my driving test, I scored 7 out of 10—luckily, the other three managed to escape!

❖ Socrates: You should take a break. You look like you need some rest.
Kat: And you look like you need a better opening line. Try again.

❖ I've been making mistakes left and right—looks like I've become a deadly *errorist*, completely unchecked!

- My wife asked, "What rhymes with 'water'?" I said, "No, it doesn't."

- I ate without paying—the food court was where justice was ultimately served!

- On my way to the optician—I'll *see* you later!

- In my quest to be eco-friendly, I wrote my diary on sandpaper at the beach—now that's a rough draft!

- My eyesight is terrible, but it doesn't bother me—my memory's so bad, I forget what I can't see!

❖ My wife complained I never buy her gifts—had no clue she owned a gift shop!

❖ In any situation, the one thing guaranteed to return home is my boomerang.

❖ I donated my piano at the Organ Donation Camp—turns out, they weren't looking for key players!

❖ My dachshund Socrates says, 'Why stand tall when you can stretch long? Horizontal is where the real magic happens!

❖ I'm such a terrible cook, grace is said after the meal.

- Want to dodge cannibals? Just tattoo 'Expired: Best Before 1995' and watch their appetites vanish!

- I wonder what sheep count when they can't sleep—probably the ever-growing crowd of drowsy humans counting them!

- There's no way to know exactly when the first watch was invented—guess time will tell.

- I told my doctor I was shrinking; he said, 'You'll just have to be a *little* patient!'

- To make a snail fast, just keep it away from food.

- ❖ People *die* every day, but I *dye* every two weeks—staying colourfully alive!

- ❖ My son wanted to see Batman, so I took him to a badminton academy. They handed me a mosquito-zapping racket, and he just nodded—lesson learned!

- ❖ They called me a bad statistician just because I said the *average* guy is downright *mean*!

- ❖ I accidentally knocked over a statue and broke it—congratulations to me on creating an award-winning *bust*!

❖ After a hard day's grind, Neolithic men unwound at the *clubhouse—* where every party was truly rocking!

❖ Two roads diverged before me—I chose the one that led to crime. I took the *psycho-path*!

❖ I'm so broke, the only binge-watching I do is on my own CCTV— live-streaming my empty fridge!

❖ I have a pen that writes *without ink—* it can write other words too!

❖ My inflatable house got punctured last night — now I'm literally living in a flat!

- ❖ I shaved my head as part of my grand strategy to cut down on *overhead* costs!

- ❖ To build a cannibal restaurant, I'm looking for someone to lend a *hand*!

- ❖ I paid for the trampoline by cheque—now both are bouncing!

- ❖ My dachshund Socrates declares, "In my dog country, non-biodegradable is non-negotiable!

- ❖ All chickens want is a world where they can cross the road without being questioned about it!

- I got my good looks from my father—he's a *plastic surgeon*!

- Being short, I've always struggled to *reach* an agreement.

- My dachshund, Socrates, says, 'Being busy doesn't mean being productive; it just means you've got a lot of barking to do—even if you're not chasing the courier guy.'

- I used to wash dishes with my wife, but then I discovered that soap and a scrubber worked much better!

- I only visit places with no bars on bars.

❖ The lump on my head is huge—my wife asked for a ring on Valentine's Day, and I asked if she meant from the landline or the mobile!

❖ The rule of Lucky Me says a dropped bottle cap will always roll to the darkest, farthest corner under the bed — precisely an inch beyond your longest reach!

❖ Do blood banks carry any interest? Oh yes — Dracula, mosquitoes, and bats are their most loyal clients!

❖ At the skin clinic, every form they gave me to fill out was a scratch card!

- ❖ I told my wife I want to be cremated—she handed me a match and said, 'Why wait?

- ❖ My dullest book sold out fast—'Buy one, suffer one free!' did the trick.

- ❖ In a fit of rage, Arthur drew his sword—so I grabbed my crayons and coloured it!

- ❖ I've heard the best watchdogs come from Switzerland—let's hope they bark on time!

- ❖ My FB says I'm an all-rounder, my résumé says future CEO — my bank account says 'bro, get a job first.'

❖ Socrates: With CCTV cameras and drones everywhere, mischief is impossible.
Kat: They should be more worried than us—innocence and honesty? We're light-years ahead on any survey!

❖ Launching my rustic furniture collection—where every scratch and dent costs extra because it's 'vintage charm.'

❖ I went to a Navy battle show. The sea was calm, no action in sight — turns out, it was a fierce submarine standoff happening *below see level*.

- They say when one door closes, another opens — in my case, that's just the issue with the car I'm trying to sell!

- Fatty food, like the sun, rises in the yeast and sets in the waist!

- I must say, the scarecrow is a brilliant creation—truly outstanding in his field!

- At IKEA, the food counter felt like a grocery store with a full kitchen kit and a manual—meals too need assembling!

❖ The delay in my solar panel installation has officially made me a light-wait champion!

❖ With my natural lack of wisdom, I count on artificial intelligence to even the odds!

❖ When you reach a fork in the road, grab it—you never know when you'll need to eat your own words!

❖ I have a step ladder, but I'm still climbing my way to finding my real ladder.

- ❖ Shakespeare and the Encyclopaedia Britannica truly shaped my youth—mostly as stepping stools to reach the hidden stash of biscuits and chocolates!

- ❖ Good steel rods are made with a-tension to detail. (Pun fully reinforced!)

- ❖ Kat: Socrates, be honest—deep down, don't you wish you were a cat?
Socrates: Never. I have self-respect… you have nine lives and no clue what to do with them.

❖ I showed up at the Emergency Room with a black eye, but one glance at my belly and they handed me a birth plan—talk about a surprise delivery!

❖ In the hot desert, when you're parched, just download a crystal-clear river—premium mirage subscription required!

❖ I guess the dinosaurs went extinct because they missed the bus—huh! The Ark!

❖ The best part of a haunted house? You're never alone, just surrounded by bad company. The worst part? The eerie soundtrack keeps reminding you of it!

❖ Drunk is when you know big words like 'inebriated' and 'intoxicated'—you just can't trust your tongue to deliver them safely!

❖ My wife has a shopping complex, and I have an inferiority complex—hers expands with every store, mine with every bill!

- ❖ Michael Jackson made the moonwalk—I always thought the moon just rolled around and called it a day... or well, night!

- ❖ Isn't it right that there aren't many ambidextrous people left?

- ❖ The job required fluency in multiple languages—I assured them I'm fluent in English, Hindi, and, when necessary, an expert in lies and refined sarcasm!

- ❖ I aimed for lateral thinking but ended up with lateral expansion—plenty of circumferential evidence to back it up!

❖ Kids thought homes only had *drawing rooms*—chickens, meanwhile, learned the hard way that butcher shops only had *dressing* rooms!

❖ In a government office, they held a slow-speed competition—red tape took first place by finishing last, undefeated as ever!

❖ My dachshund Socrates says, "Don't just sit and wait for opportunities—paw your way into them!"

❖ Count Dracula: the only guy who can pull off being a real pain in the neck.

❖ Reunions: where identifying old friends is tricky, but remembering why you became friends is the real mystery.

❖ I asked my Hindi-speaking friend whether he knew how many lives a cat has. He said '*No*,' and his friends applauded.

❖ Without the internet for days, I'd be a total vegetable—my wife's already browsing recipes.

❖ World Egg Day—an eggcellent way to crack open the day and hit the bull's-eye for health!

❖ Thanks to Microsoft and Bill, my house finally has well-installed *Windows* and secure *Gates*!

❖ Windmills have the most dedicated *fans*.

❖ Give a man a fish, he eats for a day. Teach him to fish, and you'll be cursed with endless sunset selfies and #HookedForLife posts!

❖ The past, present, and future walked into a bar — the past was drunk, the present was sipping, and the future hadn't ordered yet. The moments were grammatically tense.

❖ Socrates, my dachshund, says: 'Memories are like boomerangs — some come back gently, others whack you right between the ears!'

❖ My most boring book? It's all about drilling!

❖ I firmly believe in life after death — courtesy of my donated organs doing overtime in other people!

❖ Ever wondered: If I'm 60% water, am I technically a walking buoy, a semi-liquid snack, a confused human solution, or a mobile puddle with opinions?"

❖ Socrates: "I watched my human talk to a baby—sounded like a dog trying out a foreign accent!"
Kat: "They think it's baby talk, but to babies, it's just adults making fools of themselves."

❖ Forgetfulness: where every day is surprisingly fresh—like a reboot with no memory!

❖ A pole vaulter is just a bamboo custodian with a knack for high-stakes storage!

❖ If sheep go extinct, whom can I count on for a good night's sleep?

❖ When my wife says 'five more minutes' to get ready, I settle in for a solid nap.

❖ My recipe book of burnt offerings is now officially classified under 'Arson Studies' by the Fire and Safety Department.

❖ Even in a virtual queue, I somehow end up in the slow lane of the internet!

❖ When asked to submit my personal belongings at the counter, I proudly handed over my anger, jealousy, greed, and bloated ego—my most 'valuable' assets!

❖ A cloud with a silver lining? Sounds like a premium data storage unit.

❖ The carpenter wouldn't agree on the window rates, so I showed him the door.

❖ My bucket list was overflowing with food, so I simply renamed it my 'buffet list'

❖ I'm so absent-minded, I lose things—and the best part? I have no clue what's missing!

❖ Trying to reinvent the wheel, I went in circles—only to land right back at square one!

- ❖ My fitness app promised I'd lose 60 pounds in 6 months. I lost 100 instead—how much is that in rupees?

- ❖ I heard a mosquito boast, 'We don't just suck—we inherit! Their blood runs in our veins!'

- ❖ I claim I'm earning for future generations—just a fancy cover for my perpetual greed!

- ❖ I added 'No procrastinating' to my bucket list—but I'll get around to it later!

- ❖ Followed a YouTube *tie* tutorial in the mirror—got more *knotty* than classy!

❖ My dachshund Socrates says, 'Life is like a long walk—full of twists, turns, ups, downs, and the occasional need to stop and mark your territory!'

❖ As a blacksmith, I tried to forge ahead, shape my future, and turn my foundry into a blazing furnace of success.

❖ At the alumni get-together, I realized that the only thing aging better than wine is my ability to forget names and faces!

❖ Sent my hearing aid for repairs—no updates yet, but maybe they called!

- Synthesis—a fancy word for the research paper you write while mastering the fine art of intellectual sins!

- My dachshund Socrates says, 'Self-care is like a cozy nap in a sunny spot—skip it, and life just isn't as sweet!'

- I waited so long to meet the psychic, I became the reigning *medium wait* champion!

- They say it's the little things that matter—like the mosquito that turned my night into a horror movie.

❖ Due to the strict curfew in our area, I've decided to stay inside the box and think—don't want to risk an *out-of-the-box* violation!

❖ Socrates: If humans go more *vegan*, should we be worried?
Kat: Only if fish turns into paneer, meat into soya chunks, and bones into sugarcane sticks—what a tasteless tragedy!

❖ The avalanche turned into the ultimate rock 'n' roll performance—nature's way of bringing the house down!

- ❖ I admitted I exaggerate and lie sometimes—now they've put me in charge of the *Annual Financial Report!*

- ❖ After a stint in computers, I switched to selling hosiery—went from *hardware* to *soft-wear*!

- ❖ Taking a job at the cemetery was a grave mistake—now I'm buried in work with no way to rest in peace!

- ❖ My Kia got stolen—now it's just another mobile… No-Kia!

- ❖ Spotted a cat, and it became a leopard—big things really do come in small packages

❖ I must be Superman, doing the impossible every day—just like my mentor always said, *'Nothing is impossible!*

❖ At this rate, we'll need to celebrate Environment Day every day—just to shrink our carbon footprint to a toe print!

❖ My dachshund Socrates says, '*Unlearning* is my superpower—less knowledge, fewer mistakes, and zero guilt when I forget the rules!'

❖ With multiple personality disorder, every decision goes through a full board meeting—attended by myselves!

❖ For my wife's birthday, I handed her a box and said, "Guess what's inside!" She lit up, "A diamond necklace?" "Try again." After a few hopeful guesses, she groaned, "Ugh, a cheap pen?" She was right!

❖ My fridge says 'built-in stabilizer'—sounds like a cool place, but I still can't find it on the map!

❖ With the real intent to shed weight, I picked up a jump rope... and ended up skipping breakfast, lunch, and dinner.

❖ I have an inferiority complex—trying to simplify it so even I can understand.

❖ IIIIIIIIIIIIIIIII—looks like the barcode of someone with an overinflated ego!

❖ I wanted a good trainer for my son's tennis, so I got a horse to draw a coach—problem solved!

❖ Socrates: "I hear there are plenty of bites in the market—I'd love some samples, but my master says they're all stored in the cloud!"
Kat: "Well, if you can ever fetch from the cloud, you'll be the world's first tech-savvy dachshund!"

❖ My wife and I stepped on an oil-soaked floor—next thing you know, we were a perfect pair of slippers!

❖ I moved my home from the pole to the equator—bad idea... it melted, and now I'm officially homeless!

❖ Socrates: "Sometimes, I worry about robots taking over. What if they start doing our jobs—like being cute and cuddly?"
Kat: "Relax! Until they master the 'puppy dog eyes effect,' we've got job security."

❖ My 9-year-old disappeared after applying a cream that promised to make anyone 10 years younger—so that's why they call it vanishing cream!

- Feeling claustrophobic, I stepped outside the box—now I'm just homesick for it!

- I'm investing in bonds—starting with the best one, Casino Royale!

- Criminals were only caught red-handed after movies turned to colour—black-and-white thieves really had it easy!

- Odour! Odour! This court is now in session—onions and garlic stand accused of olfactory assault!

- Returned home after a day's work and found my family had aged 10 hours—how time flies!

- ❖ The football kept getting bigger and bigger... until reality hit me—right in the face!

- ❖ Every time I see a quarry and say, 'Ah, that's *mine*!' people assume I'm rich—when all I own is a good pun!

- ❖ That brainwashing session was so intense, I walked out slipping and sliding over the *clay* that drained out of my head!

- ❖ Dear dairy, today I failed another spelling test... but I guess I'm still mooving forward!

❖ I still can't figure out how I ended up with so many single socks—it's a sole *pair*-anormal mystery!

❖ At the hotel where breakfast was complimentary, every bite came with a flattering remark—finally, some toast that appreciates me!

❖ Socrates: "Kat, before light bulbs, what popped up when people had a brilliant idea?"
Kat: "Probably a flickering candle… or a firefly. Good thing Edison showed up — or we'd still be squinting for eureka moments in the dark!"

- ❖ I lost my suspense audiobook—now I'll never *hear* who the culprit was.

- ❖ My girlfriend dumped me for ChatGPT after realizing my love letters were AI-generated—now she's chasing DeepSeek, proving she's into artificial affection!

- ❖ Post-COVID, my wife only recognizes me with a mask on—looks like I've finally found a face she approves of!

- ❖ I've reserved a corner of my mind for unexpected thoughts—just hoping I don't misplace it like my car keys!

❖ The height of frustration? tYPING A LONG SENTENCE FAST, ONLY TO REALIZE IT ALL NEEDS TO BE REDONE.

❖ Can you show me a single person who's married? Ah, yes—every spouse at a bachelor party!

❖ I started wearing prescription glasses to bed—my dreams were getting blurry, and I couldn't read the fine print in my nightmares!

❖ It was a neck-and-neck race at the guillotine competition... but in the end, no one was left *ahead*!

❖ 90% of people are bad at math—luckily, I'm in the other 40%! Or was it 70%? Eh, whatever… I'm definitely in the smarter group!

❖ I've never been able to make a good boomerang. Mine only work on gravity—throw them straight up, and they always return… eventually!

❖ Thanks to my split personality, I can play hide-and-seek all by myself—either way, it's a win-win.

❖ The real Mission Impossible? Trying to spell it correctly after a few drinks!

❖ My wife is writing my autobiography—apparently, she knows my life better than I do! At this point, I'm just a guest appearance in my own story.

❖ My mentor told me to stop telling people more than what they need to know. Oops! I have already said too much!

❖ The exorcist vowed to banish all *spirits* — didn't know he'd clear the bar too. Ah! Now that's a horror tale!

❖ 'Never look back'—a gem of wisdom I received not from a leadership guru, a philosopher, or a psychiatrist, but from my orthopaedist… while inspecting my wrecked neck.

❖ My Google Maps lady got so frustrated with me ignoring her that she finally snapped: "100 meters ahead, pull over and ask a human for directions!"

❖ Socrates: "Kat, if you could have something over, what would it be?" Kat: "This book—before the readers start wondering why it's not!"

www.ingramcontent.com/pod-product-compliance
Lightning Source LLC
LaVergne TN
LVHW041951070526
838199LV00051BA/2978